GRANDPA ROGERS and QUEEN MARY'S FIRE

J (Johannes) Froebel-Parker

Illustrations: Ray Bono

authorHOUSE®

AuthorHouse™
1663 Liberty Drive
Bloomington, IN 47403
www.authorhouse.com
Phone: 1 (800) 839-8640

Published by AuthorHouse   04/12/2016

ISBN: 978-1-5049-8379-2 (sc)
ISBN: 978-1-5049-8378-5 (e)

Dedicated to the memory of

Rev. John (The Martyr) Rogers

1505-1555

With special thanks to

Franz Feil

Libuse Foltys

The Year of Our Lord 1555 had been a wonderful year and a horrible year, my grandmother had repeated many times. Grandfather Rogers had gone to heaven in that year, but had suffered in doing so.

Mary Tudor had been the queen of the realm and grandfather a respected preacher.

Grandmother spoke to us in English with a lovely accent from Belgium where she had been born. Before they were married, our grandfather had been a Catholic priest and had not been able to marry.

King Henry VIII of England had had six wives we learned. Divorce from Mary's mother, Catherine of Aragon, was necessary to marry the next. Queen Mary's father, Henry VIII, quarreled mightily with Catherine who refused to grant him a divorce. The Church did not permit it. So the king said the church in England would be under his leadership. He gave himself permission. In the new church Henry could remarry and priests could marry.

The Wives & Children of Henry VIII

Wife One (divorced):
CATHERINE of ARAGON
Their Child:
Mary Tudor

Wife Two (beheaded):
ANNE BOLEYN
Their Child:
Elizabeth

Wife Three (died):
JANE SEYMOUR
Their Child:
Edward

Wife Four (divorced):
ANNE of CLEVES

Wife Five (beheaded):
CATHERINE HOWARD

Wife Six (survived):
CATHERINE PARR

Grandmother taught us how to remember the fate of the six with a little ditty:

Divorced, beheaded, died: divorced, beheaded, survived.

(Catherine of Aragon, Anne Boleyn, Jane Seymour, Anne of Cleves, Catherine Howard, Catherine Parr)

"How was Grandpa Rogers able to marry you, dear Grandmother?" I asked her. My cousins listened intently as they too wondered. "Priests are not allowed to marry, but you became his wife."

She smiled as she shared her memories with us.

"Your grandfather went into holy orders in the Roman Catholic Church at the Feast of St. Stephen, 26 December 1532. Stephen was the first martyr of the Christian Faith in Jerusalem," she explained, although my cousins and I had already known about St. Stephen as our parents taught us about him every year on the day following Christmas.

Grandpa had become a priest and never thought he would marry anyone.

Two years later Grandpa moved to Antwerp in Belgium. He became a chaplain for many English merchants who lived there. "That is where he met me," our grandmother told us with a big smile. "By that time, your grandfather had met a great scholar in the Protestant faith, William Tyndale, and became a Protestant priest or *pastor*."

"Now he could marry and he asked me. I was happy to say yes!"

"My family name was a good Belgium name which in the language of the Low Countries meant *meadow* - Weyden. Your grandfather spoke Latin well and used the Latin form of Weyden-*Prata*."

"As most English people do not speak Latin he shortened the name to *Pratt*. Hence, I was Adriana de Weyden PRATT. When I married your grandfather I was then *Adriana Rogers*."

ΤΟ ΚΑΤΑ ΙΩΑΝΝΗΝ ΑΓΙΟΝ ΕΥΑΓΓΕΛΙΟΝ

Εν αρχη ην ο λογος
και ο λογος
ην προς τον θεον
και θεος ην ο λογος
ουτος ην αρχη
προς τ[ν]

Παντα δι'αυτου εγενετο
και χωρις αυτου εγενετο
ουδε εν ο γεγονεν
εν αυτω ζωη ην
και η ζωη ην
το φως των ανθρωπων

Evangelium secundum Johannem
In principio erat Verbum
et Verbum erat apud Deum
et Deus erat Verb[um]
Hoc erat in [principio]
Omnia [...]

The Gospell of Sancte John.
The fyrst Chapter.

In the begynnynge was that Worde, and that
Worde was with God: and God was thatt Worde.

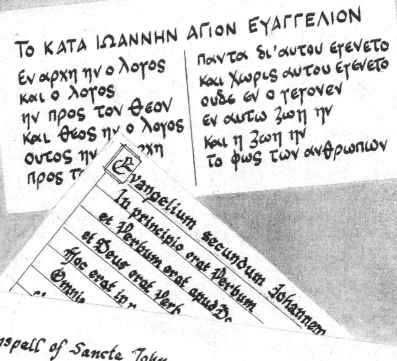

"Some of your aunts and uncles speak Flemish because they were born in Antwerp, and some speak German, because they were born in Wittenberg in Germany. Your grandfather studied with colleagues of Martin Luther."

Doctor Luther had translated the Latin version of the New Testament by the great scholar Erasmus (publisher: Johannes Ioannes Frobenius in Basel) into German for all speakers of German, Protestant and Catholic, to read.

"Your grandfather thought the same was necessary for both the Old and New Testaments to be in English."

"Einige Deiner Tanten und Onkel sprechen flämisch, weil sie in Brabant geboren sind, und manche sprechen deutsch, weil sie in Wittenberg in Deutschland geboren sind."

Großvater studierte mit Kollegen von Martin Luther. Dr. Luther hatte das Neue Testament, das der große Gelehrte Erasmus in Latein im Verlag von Johannes (Ioannes) Frobenius in Basel publizierte, in deutsch übersetzt, damit es alle Katholiken und Protestanten lesen konnten.

"Dein Großvater hielt das Gleiche für das Alte und das Neue Testament auch in englischer Sprache für erforderlich."

My family and the family of each of my cousins had a very large Bible, Old and New Testaments, bound in leather from which we read daily and more on Sundays and holidays.

This was the Bible in English which Grandfather Rogers had helped Mr. Tyndale to publish.

Mr. Tyndale was the first man to publish the New Testament in English. This was prohibited by the Church which did not want people to read it and understand it for themselves.

Grandfather's friend was executed in 1536 before he could complete the Old Testament.

Grandfather worked with his friend, Myles Coverdale, to publish the entire Bible in English.

Grandmother's uncle, Sir Jacob van Meteren, was wealthy and used his money to pay for the work and printing.

However, Grandfather knew he might be arrested so he used a made-up name, a pseudonym, or, as writers say, a "nom de plume" of "Thomas Matthews" to hide his identity.

In 1547 King Edward VI succeeded his father, King Henry VIII. He was Lutheran or Protestant also, so Grandfather returned to England in 1548. He became pastor of various congregations.

Because Grandmother was not born in England nor were her children they were not English subjects. Many of the members of Parliament were now Protestant and admired Grandfather.

They declared our family English thereby naturalizing them.

Edward was very kind and good, Grandmother told us, but he was quite ill. The royal physicians could not save him and died in 1553.

Grandfather and Grandmother were very sad. Edward had wanted his Protestant cousin, Lady Jane Grey, to be queen. He did not want his half-sisters, Mary and Elizabeth, to succeed him.

His father had broken the relationship between England and the Pope, but kept all other Catholic practices. Edward, however, had embraced the teachings of the German reformer, Dr. Martin Luther, and made the Church of England Protestant.

Grandfather would soon be in danger when on July 16, 1553 Mary became queen against Edward's wishes. Lady Jane Grey had been queen for 13 days before she too was executed.

Mary wanted to abolish the Church of England and reestablish the Catholic religion of Rome.

Grandfather spoke out against the new queen, Mary Tudor, who supported the Church of Rome. He was well known and respected, but both grandparents saw danger on the horizon.

Soon the queen called Grandfather a "heretic," a person who does not agree with the established religion.

Grandmother explained that King Phillip had admonished his wife that the execution of *heretics*, the term she used for those who did not practice her form of the Christian religion, was not helpful for her reputation and would inspire hatred for her.

King Phillip was from Spain and could not speak English.

Queen Mary, Grandmother informed us, could speak some Spanish as her mother, Catherine of Aragon, was from Spain.

Phillip was even a cousin to Mary.

His father was Charles V, Holy Roman Emperor, grandson of Queen Isabela and King Ferdinand, the Catholic Monarchs of Spain. Mary's mother, Catherine of Aragon, was their daughter.

It was a very united family, Grandmother explained. In order for King Phillip and Queen Mary to communicate they spoke a mixture of Latin, French, and Spanish:

King Phillip: *Mi querida esposa et Regina Mea: Heresis questionis de la santa iglesia. El papa en Roma n'a pas besoin de votre aide. Vos gens vont vos odiar.*

My dear wife and queen: Heresy is a matter of the Holy Church. The Pope in Rome does not need your assistance. Your people will hate you.

Meine geliebte Gattin und meine Königin: Häresie ist Klage der heiligen Kirche. Der Papst in Rom braucht Deine Hilfe nicht. Deine Leute werden Dich hassen.

Queen Mary: *Odiar? Ils devraient amarme. Je suis Regina. Je suis la protectora de la fide apostalica. Estarán confus.*

Hate? They should love me. I am the queen. I am the protectrix of the Apostalic Faith. They must be confused.

Hassen? Sie müssten mich lieben. Ich bin Königin. Ich bin die Beschützerin des apostalischen Glaubens. Sie sind verrückt.

King Phillip: *Pas de confundidos. Toutes sont Christiani y basta.*

They are not confused. They are all Christian. That is sufficient.

Keine Verrückten. Alle sind Christen und damit basta.

Queen Mary: *UNGUENTATA REGINA SUM!*

I AM AN ANOINTED QUEEN!

ICH BIN ZUR KÖNIGIN GESALBT!

King Phillip: *Tu hermano, Eduardo, quoque unguentatus fuerat. Recuerde lo que se dice en Tito 3:10:* **Hereticum hominem post unam et secundam correptionem devita.** *Il n'a pas dit MATAR.*

Your brother, Edward, was also anointed. Remember the words of Titus 3:10: A man that is an heretick after the first and second admonition reject. It does not say KILL.

Dein Bruder, Edward, war auch gesalbt. Erinnere Dich an die Worten in Titus 3:10: Einen ketzerischen Menschen meide, wenn er einmal und abermals ermahnt ist. Nirgends wird töten geschrieben.

Queen Mary: *Assez! Ya basta.*

Enough! That is enough already!

Genug! Das genügt schon!

Ignoring the advice of her husband, King Phillip of Spain, Queen Mary proclaimed that all who defied her were heretics and outlaws.

Grandpa Rogers was arrested and put in prison with others who defied Queen Mary and condemned to be burned at the stake.

His trial lasted six days.

Grandmother knelt in prayer as she learned of his condemnation.

Grandfather would be burned at the stake on February 4th.

He would be burned into ashes, so that he would have no grave for us to visit.

On the day of the execution people from all across London came to watch the spectacle in a place known as Smithfield.

Grandfather prepared himself in prayer.

The queen's representative wanted to make Grandfather suffer psychologically and wickedly told him, "I shall never pray for your soul."

However, Grandfather remembered how Jesus on the Cross had forgiven those who executed Him.

With Christian love he responded, "But, I, sir, shall pray for you, and we shall meet again in Heaven."

Grandmother and all of her eleven children including the newest one at her breast born while Grandfather was in prison stood out front among the noisy crowd.

They wanted to bring comfort to Grandpa Rogers trying hard not to cry.

One of Queen Mary's soldiers lit the torch and set ablaze the wood stacked around Grandfather who had been chained to the stake.

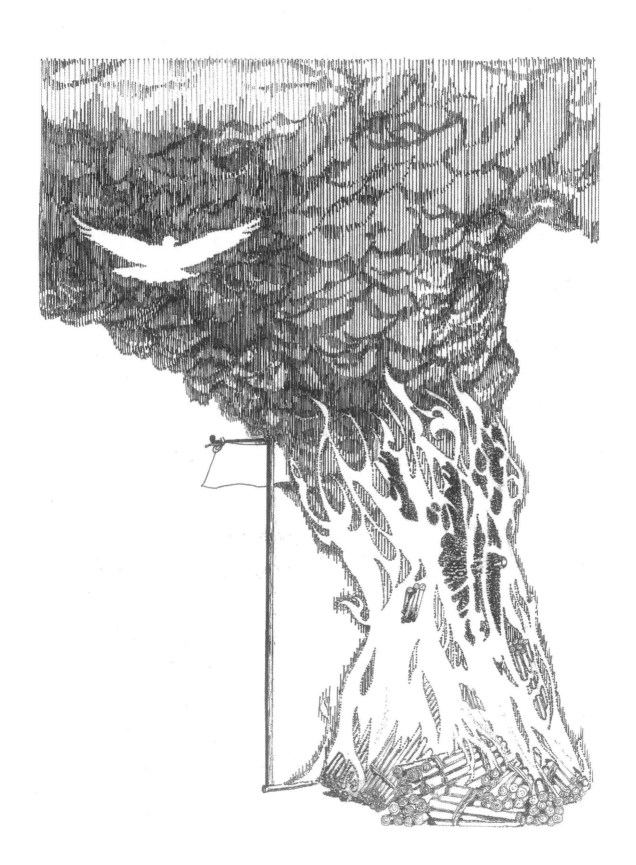

The flames rose around Grandfather, and the fire finally engulfed him completely.

The crowd gasped as a flock of doves suddenly flew up into the air swirling around and through the smoke.

Some whispered, "It is his soul being released!"

Grandmother assured her children that their father would soon be in Heaven where a kinder, gentler Queen Mary, the Mother of Jesus, would welcome him and lead him to the Throne of God.

Rev. John Rogers, 12th great grandfather to Lady Diana Spencer, 10th and 11th to author, J. Froebel-Parker and brother, Roger.